Looking at

Animals in TREES

Published by Raintree Steck-Vaughn Publishers,
an imprint of Steck-Vaughn Company

Series Editor Honor Head
Series Designer Hayley Cove
Picture Researcher Juliet Duff
Map Artwork Robin Carter / Wildlife Art Agency
Animal Symbols Arlene Adams

Raintree Steck-Vaughn Publishers Staff
Project Manager: Joyce Spicer
Editor: Pam Wells
Cover Design: Gino Coverty

Library of Congress Cataloging-in-Publication Data
Butterfield, Moira, 1961–
Animals in trees / Moira Butterfield.
p. cm. — (Looking at)
Includes index.
Summary: Introduces animals that live in trees in both temperate woods and rain forests, including squirrels, woodpeckers, fruit bats, tree boas, ocelots, and sloths.
ISBN 0-7398-0110-4 (Hardcover) ISBN 0-7398-0716-1 (Softcover)
1. Forest animals — Juvenile literature. [1. Forest animals.]
I. Title. II. Series: Butterfield, Moira, 1961– Looking at —
QL 112.B88 1999
591.73 — dc21 99-17902
CIP

Printed in China
1 2 3 4 5 6 7 8 9 0 LB 02 01 00 99

Photographic credits
Frank Lane Picture Agency: 7 S Maslowski, 8 L Lee Rue, 9 R Austing, 10 Martin Witners, 11 David Hosking, 12 Roger Wilmhurst, 13 Hugh Clark, 28 M Harvey, 29 Brake/Sunset. NHPA: 18 Kevin Schafer, 20 James Carmichael Jr., 22 Martin Wendler, 27 Stephen Dalton. Oxford Scientific Films: 6 Zig Leszczynski. Planet Earth Pictures: 14 Richard Matthews, 15, 25 Ken Lucas, 16 Claus Meyer, 17 Peter J Oxford, 19 Tom Brakefield, 21 Brian Kenney, 23 J A Provenza, 24 Ken King, 26 Carol Farneti-Foster
Cover credit Tree boa: NHPA/James Carmichael Jr.

Looking at

Animals in TREES

Moira Butterfield

Austin, Texas

www.steck-vaughn.com

Introduction

Lots of trees growing together are called forests or woods. Many forests are in cold parts of the world, where it snows almost all year long.

Some forests are hot and steamy. These are called rain forests. Here it rains a lot, but it is never cold or snowy.

Many different kinds of animals, birds, and insects live in the trees in forests and woods. They all have their own special way of finding food and shelter in trees.

Contents

Squirrel 6
Screech Owl 8
Koala 10
Woodpecker 12
Marmoset 14
Fruit Bat 16
Macaw 18
Tree Boa 20
Ocelot 22
Bush Baby 24
Tree Frog 26
Sloth 28
Where They Live 30
Index of Words to Learn . . 32

Squirrel

Squirrels live in nests in trees. The nests are high up in the trees. Squirrels have bushy tails that they use to help them balance when they climb.

Squirrels like to eat nuts, seeds, fruits, and cones. The woods are a good place for them to find food.

Screech Owl

At night screech owls fly down from their homes in the treetops to hunt for food. They have large eyes, good hearing, and sharp talons to catch field mice. The screech owl lays from three to eight eggs in a nest in a tree. It protects its nest without fear.

Koala

Koalas live in the eucalyptus trees in Australia. They munch on leaves from the branches. They never drink because they get all the juice they need from the leaves.

Newborn koalas are only one inch (2 cm) long. They live in their mother's pouch until they are big enough to travel on her back.

Woodpecker

Woodpeckers have strong beaks to peck holes in trees for their nests. They use their long, sticky tongues to scoop out bugs from under the tree bark. When a woodpecker hammers hard with its beak on a tree trunk, it makes a noise like a worker's drill.

Marmoset

Marmosets are small monkeys that live in jungles. They have very long tails. These monkeys wrap their tails around branches to help them swing through the trees.

Marmosets like to eat fruit and spiders. They use their sharp teeth to gnaw holes in trees, so sap drips out for them to drink.

Fruit Bat

These big bats are found in warm countries. They live in colonies close to trees where they can find fruit to eat. They have large eyes to see in the dark and a long nose to smell ripe fruit. They grab the fruit and crush it with their teeth to squeeze out the juice.

Macaw

These large parrots live in the rain forest. They are easy to spot because they are brightly colored and noisy. They can hold things with their claws.

Macaws use their sharp, hooked beaks to split open tasty nuts and fruits growing in trees around them.

Tree Boa

A tree boa is a long, thin green snake that lives in rain forest trees. Even its eyes are green. Its color is a good camouflage. It winds itself around a branch among the leaves, so that nothing can see it. When it is hungry, it swings out to catch passing birds to eat.

Ocelot

Ocelots are wild jungle cats. Their striped, spotted coats are good camouflage in the trees. They are expert climbers, so they easily catch birds and snakes to eat.

Baby ocelots are called kittens. They are born tiny and blind. Their mother looks after them until they grow stronger.

Bush Baby

These furry, little jungle creatures are nocturnal. That means they sleep all day and climb around the trees at night. They use their big eyes to see in the dark. To find their way in the darkness, bush babies spray scent on the trees. This way they mark their favorite paths.

Tree Frog

There are lots of different tree frogs. They have sticky pads on their toes to help them climb trees. They leap up high with their strong back legs to catch insects.

Rain forest tree frogs have bright colors and big eyes. During the day they sleep attached to the underside of a big leaf.

Sloth

Sloths spend almost all of their lives hanging upside down in the jungle trees of South America. They have long claws on each paw for gripping and climbing along branches. They move very slowly around their leafy home looking for plants to munch.

Where They Live

This map of the world shows you where the animals live.

NORTH AMERICA

squirrel

screech owl

koala

woodpecker

marmoset

fruit bat

macaw

tree boa

ocelot

SOUTH AMERICA

bush baby

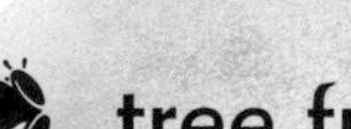
tree frog

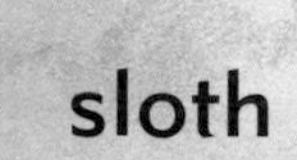
sloth

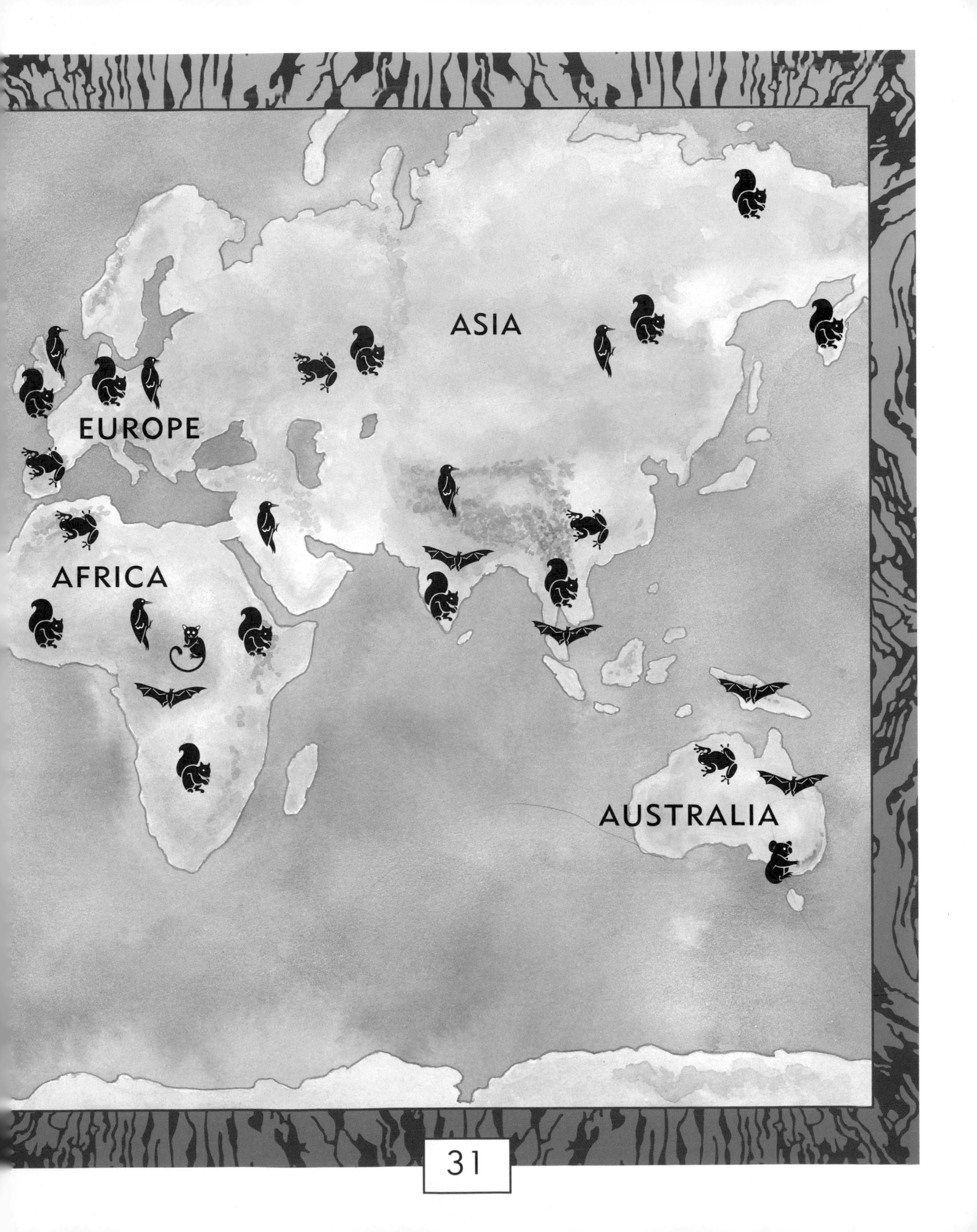
ASIA
EUROPE
AFRICA
AUSTRALIA

Index of Words to Learn

camouflage The colors and markings on an animal's coat or skin that make it hard to see. 21, 23

colony A big group living together. 17

cone The fruit of a pine or fir tree. 7

jungle Land in hot countries with lots of trees. 25, 29

pouch A stomach pocket for carrying a baby. 11

sap The juice of a tree. 15

scent A strong-smelling spray that some animals use to mark places where they have been. 25

talons Sharp claws on the end of a bird's feet. 9

BOSTON PUBLIC LIBRARY